Your
Anxiety
Journal

First published in Great Britain in 2023 by
Michael O'Mara Books Limited
9 Lion Yard
Tremadoc Road
London SW4 7NQ

A CIP catalogue record for this book is available from the British Library.

This product is made of material from well-managed, FSC®-certified forests and other controlled sources. The manufacturing processes conform to the environmental regulations of the country of origin.

ISBN: 978-1-78929-468-2 in paperback print format

1 2 3 4 5 6 7 8 9 10

Cover design by Natasha Le Coultre
Typeset by Claire Cater
Cover and internal illustrations by Charlotte Pepper
Printed and bound in China

www.mombooks.com

Your Anxiety Journal

Simple Exercises to Calm the Mind and Relieve Stress

Amy Birch   Illustrated by Charlotte Pepper

Michael O'Mara Books Limited

INTRODUCTION

Anxiety is an essential part of being human. Our anxious feelings can keep us safe by warning us of danger and alerting us to potential pitfalls. Worry can motivate us to focus and prepare, which can generate better outcomes. And it's perfectly normal for us to feel anxious during periods of high stress. Indeed, our anxiety system is one of the reasons we've been so successful as a species, driving us to make predictions about the future, reflect on the past and respond immediately to threats. But when our worries start to disrupt day-to-day life that's a sign that our anxiety response has become out of kilter. We can find ourselves stuck in a place of tension and fear, where worst-case scenarios are always looming and we are disconnected from our own power to cope.

It's not surprising that in recent years many of us have been living with a greater degree of anxiety. Perhaps you've found that your feelings of anxiety are very strong or last a long time. You might be avoiding situations that cause you to feel anxious or sense that your fears are out of proportion with the situation. This book is filled with ways to understand how you experience anxiety and suggestions for what you can do to help. There are exercises on dialling down anxiety levels in the moment, recognizing and tackling unhelpful patterns, and building habits that can help to prevent anxiety from taking hold. There's also lots of space for your own reflections on how you can support yourself. Use the exercises as a starting point and see what works for you.

If at any point you feel in need of further support, turn to the 'Resources' section at the back of the book, where you'll find useful websites, helplines and more.

'He who knows others is wise; he who knows himself is enlightened'

LAO TZU

OBSERVE

The way we experience anxiety is individual to each of us. We may share similar ingredients but the exact recipe will be unique to you. Investigating your own recipe gives you vital insight into not only how you personally experience anxiety but also how you can best help yourself. You'll be able to see what's working for you, what's not and the kinds of strategies that might be a good fit.

When we're struggling we often try to get through as best we can; we're relieved when the struggle's over and happy to just move on. It makes a lot of sense but it also means that we're missing out on the opportunity to learn and make changes in the future.

Treat this as a data capture exercise, recording information about what happens when your feelings of anxiety spike, how they are maintained and how they recede. It might seem like a lot of effort, especially if you experience many anxiety spikes during the day, but you only need to keep it up for a week or two to gather a meaningful amount of data, and the rewards will be worth it.

You don't have to fill this in while you're in the middle of the situation, but it can be a good idea to have a go soon after, once you're more relaxed, so the memory is fresh.

Situation: When did the anxious feelings start? Where were you, what were you doing and who were you with?

Feelings: How did you feel? Name the emotions.

Strength: How strong were the feelings? Grade them out of ten (turn to 'Grade It' on page 16 for more on this).

Physical Sensations: How did it feel in your body? You might have noticed changes such as an increase in your heart rate or breathing, tension in particular parts of your body, perspiration or digestive discomfort.

Thoughts and Images: What thoughts or images were going through your mind?

Response: What did you do? How did you try to cope? And how did you feel once you'd done this?

Strength: Did your response influence your feelings? Grade them out of ten again and compare to the previous number.

If you think about these questions each time your anxiety spikes, you'll get a clearer sense of what situations trigger it and how you experience it both physically and mentally. You'll also begin to see how particular thoughts and images contribute to maintaining your anxious feelings. Importantly, you'll be able to reflect on what you do when you're feeling anxious and to what degree those responses help.

Situation: _____
_____
_____

Feelings: _____
_____
_____

Strength: /10

Physical Sensations: _____
_____
_____

Thoughts and Images: _____
_____
_____

Response: _____
_____
_____

Strength: /10

Situation: _____

_____

_____

Feelings: _____

_____

_____

Strength: /10

Physical Sensations: _____

_____

_____

Thoughts and Images: _____

_____

_____

Response: _____

_____

_____

Strength: /10

13

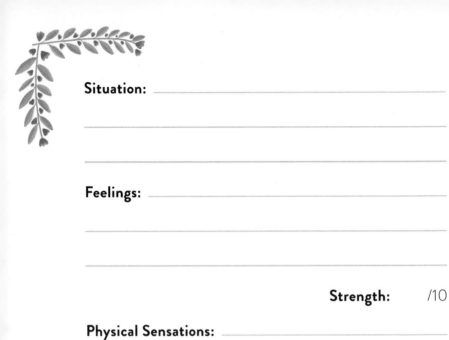

Situation: _____
_____
_____

Feelings: _____
_____
_____

Strength: /10

Physical Sensations: _____
_____
_____

Thoughts and Images: _____
_____
_____

Response: _____
_____
_____

Strength: /10

Situation: _____

_____

_____

Feelings: _____

_____

_____

Strength: /10

Physical Sensations: _____

_____

_____

Thoughts and Images: _____

_____

_____

Response: _____

_____

_____

Strength: /10

GRADE IT

Just as each of us experiences anxiety in our own way, so different techniques will be more or less helpful. One way of finding out what works for you is to rate your anxiety level before doing the technique or exercise and then again immediately after. By comparing the levels using the grading system on the following pages, you'll be able to see how impactful that particular exercise is for you.

Keep in mind that some techniques take practice. So what at first might be only a small difference could grow with time and repetition. You might also find that certain techniques are better suited to particular situations.

First you need to set your scale. To do this, you'll need to recall a particular time that you would rate 10 out of 10 in terms of anxiety. You don't need to engage with the memory in any detail, just remember the occasion and give it a brief title, something like 'Exam Day' or 'Holiday Flight'. Then write this title down next to the 10 on page 20.*

* If you found recalling this memory difficult or destabilizing you might like to try the next exercise, 'Safe and Secure', to re-ground you in the safety of the present.

Next, think of a time when you have felt at your most relaxed, totally at peace, and give that memory its own brief title. Make a note of it next to the 0 on page 20.

Now, think of a time when your anxiety level was pretty much in the middle of these two extremes, and, again, give it a brief title. Pop this one next to the 5.

Now you have your own personalized anxiety scale.

As well as using it to measure and compare how well particular strategies work for you, you can also use the scale to help you recognize how different situations impact your level of anxiety. For instance, it's not uncommon to feel as if we've had very high anxiety all day. But if you were to regularly check your anxiety against the scale you may find that it fluctuates throughout the day, with both low and high points. Turn back to the 'Observe' exercise to see how you can use the scale to learn more about how you experience anxiety.

10. _____

9. _____

8. _____

7. _____

6. _____

5. _____

4. _____

3. _____

2. _____

1. _____

0. _____

SAFE AND SECURE

When we're feeling anxious we can find ourselves getting stuck inside our head, often spun up in worries or thoughts about the past or future. These grounding techniques use your body to bring you back into the world and into the present. They remind you that in this moment you are safe and secure. They are designed to help you regain a sense of calm and so are particularly helpful when you're feeling overwhelmed or panicky. They can be used nearly anywhere, any time.

Safe and Stable: Sit upright on a chair with your feet flat on the floor. Take a few slow deep breaths as you notice your weight pressing against the seat. Move your attention down your legs and into your feet. Notice how they meet the ground and the ground pushes back up to keep you stable and secure. Keep your attention on this sense of stability while you continue to breathe slowly and deeply.

Hand Clasp: Take one hand in the other and clasp them together firmly. Feel the strength in your grip, the strength that comes from within you. Hold your hands like this for about a minute.

Senses: Describe in detail three things that you can see. Describe two things that you can touch. Describe one thing that you can hear. You can do this out loud, in your head or you can write it down.

Breathe Out Tension: Close your eyes and take a few deep breaths. Notice anywhere that you're holding tension in your body, such as in your shoulders, jaw or temples. As you continue to breathe deeply, imagine that tension softening and melting away, like candle wax being gently heated.

Doodle a Calming Image: Choose a calming image, such as a sun, tree or cat, and make a very simple drawing here. Notice the sensation of your pen or pencil on the paper, the sound it makes as it skims the surface, how the pigment is deposited on the paper and the colours and texture that it leaves. Repeat the drawing as many times as you like.

RELAXED BREATHING

When we are stressed, anxious or tense our breathing can become rapid and shallow, like it does when we exercise. Which makes a great deal of sense when you consider that one of the primary roles of our anxiety system is to prime us to take action – that 'fight or flight response' that you may have heard of. It's perfectly normal but, given that the situations that cause us anxiety these days don't often require us to fight or run, this physiological reaction doesn't get to serve its original purpose. In fact, this short, shallow breathing sends messages to our brain and body that the danger is still present and that our anxiety system needs to remain switched on. And if you don't realize that it's happening it may fuel your anxious state without you even knowing.

Exercise can be an effective means of reducing anxiety as it gives that flight or fight response an outlet. However, it's not always possible to hit the gym when we notice our anxious feelings starting to rise, which is why breathing exercises are so useful. Slowing and deepening your breathing can be a very effective method of interrupting that anxious cycle. Regular, slower breaths communicate to our brain and body that we are safe, that the danger is over and we can relax.

There are lots of breathing techniques that you can try, but sometimes the simple ones are the best. The idea here is to learn the skill of relaxed breathing.

To get a sense of what you're aiming for, first experiment with noticing the difference between tense and relaxed breathing. Do this when you are not feeling anxious.

1 | Place one hand on your belly and one on your chest.

2 | Using just the top of your lungs and ribcage, draw in air. Keep your breaths short and shallow. You'll notice that only the hand on your chest rises and falls. Keep this up for a few breaths and think about how it feels.

3 | Now breathe in using your stomach and diaphragm. This time, you'll notice the hand on your belly moving and the one on your chest staying relatively still. Draw in the air deeply and slowly. Keep this up for a few breaths and notice how it feels.

It is these slower, deeper breaths that you're aiming for with your relaxed breathing practice – and practice is most definitely the key. Aim for a handful of times a day, taking at least a few minutes each time. Not only does this help to bring calm to your day, it will also mean you feel comfortable and confident using it as a strategy for calming anxiety when you need it.

Here are the principles of relaxed breathing:

1 | Breathe in and out through your nose.

2 | Do so slowly and evenly.

3 | Find a pace that feels comfortable. You could start by breathing in for a slow count of three and out for a slow count of three. Over time you might find that you can take even slower breaths.

4 | Practise while lying down at first, then, when you feel more confident, move to a sitting position and then standing.

5 | Put reminders in your phone or diary, or link your relaxed breathing practice to another established habit, such as brushing your teeth in the morning and at night.

6 | Keep it up for a minute or two each time. Extend the time as you become more confident.

'You cannot
perceive beauty
but with a
serene mind'

HENRY DAVID THOREAU

EXPRESS YOURSELF

Whether through talking to someone you trust or writing in this very journal, expressing your feelings and thoughts can be an effective and simple means of defusing an anxious state. By verbalizing our worries or writing them down, we do a number of things:

1| We externalize the worries. By getting them out of our minds and into the world we can experience relief, in the same way that a pressure-release valve works.

2| We can hear ourselves more clearly. When we put our thoughts and feelings into words they take a definite shape and we can better understand what's going on and what we might need.

3 | We open up to different perspectives – whether that's the feedback we get from the person we're talking to or even just ourselves when we read back our own words.

4 | We look further on than our thoughts allow. When we worry we often get stuck at a particular point – often the worst part – and rather than trying to figure out what we could do to manage the situation and move forward, we cycle back to the beginning and go through the same worries over and over. (Take a look at 'Turn the Page' on page 106 for more on this.)

5 | We can see the limit to the worry. Feeling anxious can make it hard to get a clear idea of just what we're dealing with, and the experience of the worry itself can feel never-ending. In communicating exactly what we

are worried about we enclose it. It is held within the words. When we write down our worry, we can see the white of the paper surrounding the words like a boundary. And we can put a full stop to show that there is an end. We create clarity, a limit and an ending. This can help it to feel less overwhelming and more manageable.

6 | When the worry is out there in front of us we can choose what to do with it. We are able to decide whether our anxious reaction is alerting us to something that we can do something about or whether it's a familiar worry that we know from experience does not need directly addressing. We can then make a decision about what to do, whether that's problem solving or using strategies to reduce our anxious sensations.

'Fill your
paper with the
breathings of
your heart'

WILLIAM WORDSWORTH

BETTER OUT THAN IN

Writing down your worries can be an effective means of freeing up head space, especially when you need it for something else. For instance, this technique can be particularly useful in disrupting those sleep-sapping 3 a.m. worry spirals.

You can keep the writing to short bullet points or go into a bit more detail. Find out what works for you. The key is to be intentional about it. Take a few deep breaths before you start and then a couple more when you're finished.

Some people find it helpful to keep a notebook and pen next to their bed. If you're out and about you could keep notes on your phone. When you've finished writing, close the notebook or put your phone out of sight for a while. The point is to put away the worries. But you might find that the anxious part of you wants to revisit them, even after you've written them down. See if you can reassure that part from a compassionate place. For instance, you could tell it that it's done its job in alerting you and can stand down now. There's nothing more you need to do. You'll come back to these worries when you can address them fully.

Remember to come back to the list at some point. Choose a time when you're feeling relaxed. You might want to try out the 'Designated Worry Time' exercise on page 60. At this point, you can assess the worries and whether you need to take any action.

Once you've done this exercise several times, it can be useful to look back through the lists of worries in case you can identify any patterns, such as common themes or thinking errors (the next exercise, 'Tangled Thinking', explains more about this). Are there any insights that might help you better support yourself in the future?

'What a comfort is this journal. I tell myself to myself and throw the burden on my book and feel relieved'

ANNE LISTER

TANGLED THINKING

You might have already come across the idea of 'thinking errors'. Or you might have heard them called 'skewed thinking', 'thinking biases' or 'cognitive distortions'. These terms all refer to how we sometimes don't see things as they really are. They're very common and most of us make thinking errors now and again, but when they become habitual they exaggerate our anxiety by distorting reality and making things seem worse than they are.

Distorted thinking tends to run along common themes. Have a look through the list here and see if any chime with you. The more you can identify your own common thinking errors the more you'll be able to catch them when they start up. The 'Evidence Check' on page 51 can be a useful way of addressing thinking errors when they come up.

'The greatest discovery of my generation is that a human being can alter his life by altering his attitudes of mind'

WILLIAM JAMES

Catastrophizing: When we make negative predictions about the future, often looking at the worst-case scenario instead of the far more likely outcomes. Example: 'My friend is late. What if her car crashed?!'

All-Or-Nothing Thinking: When we see the situation in black and white and miss the grey in the middle. Example: 'If I don't do this perfectly, I'm a total failure.'

Disqualifying the Positive: When we dismiss positive evidence and find a way for positives not to count. Example: 'Yeah, I got good feedback, but I bet everybody did.'

Mind Reading: When we believe we know what others are thinking while dismissing contradictory evidence. Example: 'They think I'm stupid and can't do anything.'

Labelling: When we categorize ourselves or others, simplifying them in an unhelpful way. Example: 'They're a bad person.'

Emotional Reasoning: When we believe something must be true because we feel like it is, ignoring contradictory evidence. Example: 'I feel self-conscious so everyone must be looking at me.'

Mental Filtering: When we focus exclusively on negative aspects and miss the positives: 'Someone said they didn't like my picture; I must be terrible at photography.' (While ignoring all the positive comments.)

Magnifying/Minimizing: When we magnify the negative or minimize the positive. Example: 'That last piece of feedback proves how rubbish I am at my job. Just because I hit my end-of-year goals doesn't mean I'm actually any good.'

Overgeneralizing: When we make sweeping conclusions that go far beyond what's currently going on, often using language like 'always', 'never', 'everything' and 'nothing'. Example: 'Typical me, something always goes wrong.'

Personalization: When we believe we are to blame when bad things happen, missing more likely explanations. Example: 'My partner's really upset, it must be my fault.'

Conditional Thinking: When we think in 'shoulds' and 'musts' and overestimate the negative consequences if we do not meet these rules. Example: 'I should not need help.'

EVIDENCE CHECK

Thoughts or ideas that cause us to feel anxious can often feel like facts. Indeed, it's because we have a strong emotional reaction that we believe them: they feel true. But often it's more a reflection of how we feel about the thought itself. For instance, you might have the thought 'I will never get this piece of work done'. The idea that this is true might feel horrible, but it doesn't necessarily mean it is factually correct.

This exercise is about testing our anxious thoughts in a scientific manner. The point here is not to try to convince yourself to take a more positive mindset but rather to keep a genuinely open mind as you discover what the evidence reveals.

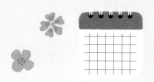

The first step is to write down the thought in the form of a statement. For instance 'I will never get this piece of work done' or 'nobody likes me'.

Next, consider how much you currently believe it. Rate your level of belief out of ten – ten if you believe it completely and zero if you don't believe it at all. Make a note of that number.

The next step is to collect all the evidence that confirms the statement. Make a note of everything you come up with in the left-hand column of the table on page 56. Remember that you're looking for evidence and that means facts: what you know to be true, not what you believe or feel. Consider past experiences and outcomes.

'I can shake off everything as I write; my sorrows disappear, my courage is reborn'

ANNE FRANK

When you've compiled as much evidence as you can, move on to the next column and start listing all the evidence that does not support that statement.

If, as you're filling in the table, you find yourself tempted to use assumptions or predictions as evidence, see if you can spot any thinking errors (see the previous exercise, 'Tangled Thinking').

When you've finished, read through all the evidence that you've collated. Now look back to the original statement and consider how much you believe it now. Give it a rating out of ten, just like you did at the start.

If the number has changed, how might you update the original statement to be more accurate? Don't worry if your alternative statement is a bit longer than the original – the reality tends to be more nuanced than our anxious thoughts. What other ways of looking at the situation might there be? List out the alternative possibilities. Sometimes it helps to imagine what you might say to a friend if they were in the same situation.

Original Statement: _____

_____

Belief Level: /10

Evidence For:

_____

_____

_____

_____

_____

_____

_____

Evidence Against:

_____

_____

_____

_____

_____

_____

_____

Alternative Statement: _____

_____

Belief Level: /10

Original Statement: _____

_____

Belief Level: /10

Evidence For: **Evidence Against:**

_____   _____

_____   _____

_____   _____

_____   _____

_____   _____

_____   _____

Alternative Statement: _____

_____

Belief Level: /10

Original Statement: _____

_____

Belief Level: /10

Evidence For: | **Evidence Against:**

_____   _____

_____   _____

_____   _____

_____   _____

_____   _____

_____   _____

Alternative Statement: _____

_____

Belief Level: /10

Original Statement: _____

_____

Belief Level: /10

Evidence For: | **Evidence Against:**

_____ | _____

_____ | _____

_____ | _____

_____ | _____

_____ | _____

_____ | _____

Alternative Statement: _____

_____

Belief Level: /10

DESIGNATED WORRY TIME

Worries can be very demanding. They claim our attention whenever they pop into our minds and insist that we attend to them immediately. That can be quite disruptive if it happens a lot. Also, sometimes addressing them immediately, even though that comes with the promise of relief, can be counter-productive in the long term. We end up training ourselves that all our worries *need* to be addressed immediately, that they are urgent and we can't be OK unless we resolve them now. And many worries aren't easily resolved, so instead this demand for our attention just keeps us busy worrying.

If this sounds familiar then you might try experimenting with setting designated worry times to help to break that cycle of attention and urgency. Each day, assign a block of time to address your worries – at first, it can be helpful to have a couple of slots per day. Try to do it at the same time every day so that the practice becomes regular and predictable. Choose a start time and end time. Ten minutes might be enough or you might need longer. Pick a time when there won't be any additional pressures or distractions.

Then, throughout the day, when worries pop into your mind, note them down somewhere, such as in a notebook or on your phone. Consciously decide to leave the worries there and remind yourself that you will address them when you can give them your full focus. You might find it helpful to thank that anxious feeling for making you aware of these concerns. Then close the notebook or put your phone away and carry on with whatever you were doing. When you first start this practice the worry may continue to demand your attention. Just notice that's happening and, as best as you can, bring your attention back to the present. You might find it helpful to try one of the distraction methods in the next exercise.

When the time comes for your designated worry time, start it with conscious intent. Make sure you are in a calm space. You might want to take a few deep breaths before you start. Take out your notes and work through them. Consider how you feel about each of the worries. Are they as distressing now as when they first popped into your mind? If they are, you might like to use one of the other exercises in this book during your worry time, such as 'Evidence Check' on page 51 or 'Scenario Spectrum' on page 113.

Remember to set an end point to your worry time and stick to it. Some people find it helpful to use a timer. When you are finished, close your notebook, get up from your seat and do something else. You might like to finish it with some relaxing breathing or other soothing exercise. It can be helpful to already have planned what you'll do afterwards before you sit down. Make the transition into and out of worry time clear and deliberate.

DISTRACTION

As we've seen, dwelling on worried thoughts,
particularly when they are not the kind that can
be resolved, often escalates our sense of anxiety.
Distraction is a simple and effective means of
interrupting that cycle; by refocusing our attention,
we disengage from unhelpful thought spirals and
allow our anxiety response to subside.

The good news is that we can actually only focus
our conscious attention on one thing at a time. That
means that if you fill your attention with something
else then there isn't any spare for unhelpful worries.

Physical activity is one of the most immediate
methods of distraction. That might be in the shape

of exercise, such as going out for a jog, but it can also be less sweaty, such as running errands or doing chores.

Of course, it's not always possible to be physically active when we're feeling anxious so you can also try refocusing your attention. Refocusing might be as simple as engaging in a conversation, reading something you find interesting or actively listening to music. It just needs to be something that's genuinely absorbing. Find what works best for you.

Or, if you're out and about you could consider using your different senses. People-watching can be a good one. Choose someone who looks interesting and make up a story about what they're doing that day, give them an elaborate backstory. Or you could tune into the sounds that surround you and try to pick out each individual strand.

Creative pursuits are another a great source of distraction, whether that's writing, drawing, playing music or anything else that you find engrossing. Use the following pages as your blank canvas. Or you could try colouring in the pattern on the page opposite. Many people find intricate colouring a deeply relaxing and distracting activity.

Different distraction techniques work best in different situations so keep experimenting.

Be mindful that your distraction techniques don't turn into avoidance. When we avoid things that cause us to feel anxious we are reinforcing the message that the subject of our worries is dangerous and that we are not able to cope with it. Aim to use distraction as a means of dropping unproductive worries in the moment rather than as an escape from fears that could be effectively addressed (turn to 'Step by Step' on page 74 for more on this).

'I prefer to be
true to myself,
even at the hazard
of incurring the
ridicule of others,
rather than to be
false, and to incur my
own abhorrence'

FREDERICK DOUGLASS

STEP BY STEP

Avoiding what makes us feel anxious is a really common and understandable way of coping. The problem is that avoidance can actually work to maintain fear. We miss out on the chance to challenge assumptions we've developed about the fear or expand our confidence while tackling the problem. Instead, we teach ourselves that this is not only something we should be fearful of but also something that we can't cope with. The fear grows and we feel less and less capable and more reliant on avoiding it all together.

Not that you need to jump straight in. People with phobias of snakes, for example, don't rid themselves of fear by being confronted by a giant anaconda. That just creates panic. What's needed is a slow – sometimes very slow – process of exposure and confidence-building. This way, you make small, steady steps, tackling your fear in manageable chunks.

Using the snake example, your first step might be looking at a photo of a snake. If a photo of a real snake feels too much then perhaps that needs to be step two, and step one could be starting with a picture of a cartoon snake. Each step should cause a bit of discomfort at first but at a level that you can cope with. After a few minutes, the sensation of fear should subside a bit. You might want to use a relaxation technique, such as relaxed breathing, to help you to feel calm. Repeat the step each day until you feel confident and comfortable then move on to the next one. If that step turns out to be too ambitious, update your plan with extra steps until you're able to face the fear in full.

If you have a particular fear that you're avoiding try mapping out a step-by-step plan here. Start by setting the end point that you want to reach, then you know what you're building up to. Remember to be patient and compassionate with yourself. Your fear took time to develop so it makes sense to give yourself time to change it.

End Point: _____

Step 1: _____

Step 2: _____

Step 3: _____

Step 4: _____

Step 5: _____

End Point: _____

Step 1: _____

Step 2: _____

Step 3: _____

Step 4: _____

Step 5: _____

End Point: _____

Step 1: _____

Step 2: _____

Step 3: _____

Step 4: _____

Step 5: _____

End Point: _____

Step 1: _____

Step 2: _____

Step 3: _____

Step 4: _____

Step 5: _____

'It is not because
things are difficult
that we do not dare;
it is because we do
not dare that they
are difficult'

SENECA

CULTIVATE YOUR INPUTS

Our brains are incredible data-processing machines. They act like sponges, soaking up information about everything around us. It is worth giving some thought to what you actively bring your brain into contact with and what impact it might be having on you. In particular, think about your phone and other digital devices. They are filled with content that's designed to elicit an emotional response in order to keep our attention.

You could think about frequency as well as the content itself. Many of us reach for our phone when we're having a break or looking for a distraction without consciously realizing we're giving our brain a good soaking in the content that pops up. For instance, you might enjoy being clued into what's going on in the news, but what was once reading a newspaper for half an hour in the morning has become a habit of checking and rechecking your phone throughout the day.

Try keeping a log of your particular inputs, when you turn to them and how they impact your mood. Once you've got some useful data you could consider what changes (if any) you'd like to try.

It's worth clarifying that cultivating your inputs isn't the same as avoidance; rather it's about pro-actively making choices about what you let into your life. Crucially, it comes from a place of empowerment rather than fear.

Type of Input: _____

When and Where: _____

_____

How Do You Feel Afterwards? _____

_____

_____

_____

Type of Input: _____

When and Where: _____

_____

How Do You Feel Afterwards? _____

_____

_____

_____

Type of Input: _____

When and Where: _____

_____

How Do You Feel Afterwards? _____

_____

_____

_____

Type of Input: _____

When and Where: _____

_____

How Do You Feel Afterwards? _____

_____

_____

_____

'Instruction
does much, but
encouragement
everything'

JOHANN WOLFGANG VON GOETHE

THE CHEERLEADER IS
MIGHTIER THAN THE CRITIC

When something doesn't go to plan, how does being criticized make you feel? What does it do to your confidence? To your willingness to give it another go? To your attitude to yourself?

Now imagine the setback is met with curiosity, compassion and encouragement instead. Again, ask yourself: How does it make me feel? What does it do to my confidence? To my willingness to give it another go? To my attitude to myself?

The critic who merely points out faults and negative consequences creates a dead-end. Without curiosity, there's no space to understand what happened or how to make changes in the future. Without compassion, there's no recognition that you're a person not a robot. And without encouragement, there's no fuel to try again.

How often do you criticize or blame yourself? If you noticed that one of your thinking errors was personalization – thinking you are always the one to blame when bad things happen, missing more likely explanations – then this exercise may be particularly useful. Over the next week, see if you can spot when you start to criticize yourself and keep a note of the circumstances, what you're criticizing yourself for, and any feelings or thoughts that come up as a result. Knowing your self-critic patterns will help you catch them in the future. You might like to try the 'Evidence Check' exercise on some of these thoughts about yourself. You could also note down some ideas about how you might be able to offer yourself curiosity, compassion and encouragement in the future.

If you're not used to responding to yourself in this way, it may well feel alien or uncomfortable at first, particularly the encouragement. But that only means there's more reason to practise and to find your own encouraging voice: avoid platitudes or clichés; imagine that you're speaking to a friend; write what you mean.

'Because when
you are imagining,
you might as well
imagine something
worth while'

L. M. MONTGOMERY

WHEN THINGS GO WELL

In the last exercise, you got to know your inner critic. While you were keeping an ear out for when it pipes up, did you notice it having anything to say when things went well? Strangely, we are often far more likely to blame ourselves for negative outcomes than for positive ones. According to this perspective, we are only responsible for the bad stuff and have little or nothing to do with the good. In fact, we might not even notice the good, let alone our own part in bringing it about.

When you consider the purpose of our anxiety system – to look out for potential dangers – it makes a lot of sense to see the world in this limited way. But if we keep up this view even when situations are not dangerous then we get a very one-sided picture of our world, meaning we end up missing a great deal – that means neutral events as well as positive ones.

Think back over the past day. It can help to break it down into small periods of time so you don't accidentally skip over useful information. Ask yourself what went well or what went to plan. Use the space on pages 95–6 to keep a record. As you go, check in to see what your part was in that achievement. It might not be anything extraordinary – in fact, it will probably be pretty mundane given that yesterday was likely an average day – but where you influenced the outcome, make a note of that too.

See if you can catch any minimizing, dismissive or discounting thoughts as you go. For instance, if you noted down that you got to work on time, your inner critic might pipe up to say: 'Yeah, but people do that every day, that's nothing special.' First, consider how accurate that is. If you're someone who's often late then that is actually something special. And if it isn't unusual for you, it's still something that worked well. Remember, you're not asking for a medal, just recognizing that it happened.

IMAGINE YOUR WAY

TO RELAXATION

Imagination is a powerful tool. Elite athletes, for instance, routinely use visualizations to improve their performance. The mental training actually influences their physical ability.

One way to use your imagination when managing feelings of anxiety is to visualize yourself into a place of relaxation.

1 | Sit in a comfortable position with your eyes closed.

2 | Allow your breath to slow and deepen as you relax into the chair.

3 | Conjure an image of a relaxing place in your mind. It can be somewhere you've been before or a completely made-up space. The key is that it feels comfortable, safe and relaxing.

4 | Don't worry if you become distracted – you almost certainly will and that's absolutely fine. Just notice that your mind has wandered and, with the next few breaths, guide it back to your image.

5 | Use your senses to enhance the experience. What colours can you see, what shapes? How bright is it? What can you hear? What can you touch? How does it feel? Are there any smells? Any tastes?

6 | Spend as much time as you want in this restful place. It might be a few minutes, it might be half an hour.

7 | When you've finished, open your eyes and sit quietly for another couple of minutes before getting up.

You can now return to this restful place whenever you need to. Like with any technique, the more you practise, the easier it becomes. You might want to work it into your daily routine, perhaps before bed, to build up your practice in a calm and peaceful space. That way, it'll become increasingly familiar and accessible, and a useful on-the-go tool to bring down levels of anxiety when you need it most.

Over time, you might like to enrich the imaginary experience even further. Perhaps you'd like to walk about in your restful place? Or is there a relaxing activity that you'd like to do, such as skimming stones, gardening or knitting with yarn?

Sometimes you'll find that a particular visualization doesn't work in quite the way you'd hoped. In which case, think about what feels relaxing to you. For instance, if you relax by hiking you could conjure the route of a favourite walk. You might even imagine yourself taking a break at a particularly picturesque spot and enjoying a thermos of something warming.

FUN

We know that we can bring down our anxiety levels with relaxation, but what sometimes gets lost is that relaxing doesn't have to be all about breathing exercises and yoga and seriousness. It can also be about fun, silliness and laughter. Adults aren't often encouraged to be playful, but maybe it would help if we were.

Think about what makes you feel light-hearted and write down everything that pops into your mind here. Think about activities, people, scenarios,

books, TV, films – anything at all. No editing, just get it down.

Once you've got all your ideas down, read them back (remember, no judging) and think about how you might work some of them into your life a little more. Even better would be to start making plans right now for something that you can do this week.

It's all too easy to forget about fun in the busy tumult of the everyday, so you might want to copy out the list onto a separate piece of paper and stick it somewhere you'll see it regularly, such as on your fridge or wardrobe door, as a reminder.

'What soap is
to the body,
laughter is
to the soul'

JEWISH PROVERB

TURN THE PAGE

Sometimes worries can take the form of 'what if . . .': 'What if I get fired? What if I get sick? What if my friend doesn't like me?'

The interesting thing about these sorts of worries, which can tend towards worst-case scenario thinking, is that they give an artificial ending; they aren't the whole story. Instead, they create a cliffhanger. And cliffhangers are designed to leave you in limbo, in a state of uncertainty and high stress.

One way of addressing these sorts of worries is to actually continue the story. Instead of testing the validity of the worry, you take the stance of 'OK, so what if this does actually happen? What do you do next? And after that? And how about after that?'

What would you do if the thing you're
worried about actually did come to pass?

How would you cope?

Have you had to manage
anything like this before?

What did you do in the past that was helpful?

How did you take care of yourself?

What resources are available to you?
Think about people, sources of support
and your own personal strengths.

This way, you turn the page of the story, move past
the cliffhanger which keeps you in a stressed and
helpless place, and re-engage with your own power
to deal with the situation.

Writing the story down can be especially effective
to help you to stay focused and moving forward. It
also creates a record that you can turn back to when
you need to. This may be helpful if your particular
'what if . . .' is a common worry for you. If you find
yourself catastrophizing as you work through the
story you might want to try the next exercise,
'Scenario Spectrum'.

'I am an old man
and have known
a great many
troubles, but most
of them have never
happened'

PROVERB

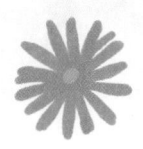

SCENARIO SPECTRUM

By now, you'll be used to the idea of your anxiety system operating like a filter on the world. Because its job is to look out for danger, when we're facing uncertainty our anxiety system can kick in and our attention becomes tuned into only a small section of the spectrum of possible outcomes – that means the bad ones, as we see them. As a system for avoiding dangers at all costs that makes sense – the 'better safe than sorry' philosophy. But if your anxiety system is switched on a lot of the time then that can become exhausting. And if it is poor at predicting outcomes or your ability to deal with situations then you can be left with a skewed view of the world and yourself.

One way to start to educate your anxiety system is to guide your attention back to the rest of the spectrum of outcomes.

The thing about uncertainty is that when we don't know what's going to happen all outcomes are still open. This means that the worst-case scenario is a possibility – but so is the best-case scenario, and, crucially, so are all of the myriad OK-ish scenarios swimming about in the middle.

The next time you are facing uncertainty and feel your anxious feelings starting to rise, try this exercise.

1 | Write down the worst-case scenario on the far left-hand side of the spectrum on the next page.

2 | Now think about what the very best-case scenario might be and make a note of that on the far right-hand side of the spectrum.

3 | Now you have the polar outcomes clearly in front of you, but there's going to be a whole spread of possible outcomes in the middle. Start filling them in. You'll probably have to switch gears in your mind as these outcomes are likely to be less emotionally provocative and more mundane. They're the more hum-drum, the more everyday, and that means they tend to be the more realistic.

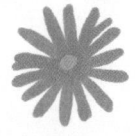

**Worst-case
Scenario:**

**Worst-case
Scenario:**

**Worst-case
Scenario:**

116

→

→

→ **Best-case Scenario:**

→

→

→ **Best-case Scenario:**

→

→

→ **Best-case Scenario:**

DEBRIEF

While many of our worries are future-focused, we don't tend to take the time to consider how accurate our powers of prediction actually are. And if we do, we can dismiss positive outcomes as flukes, explain them away or just ignore them altogether.

Try this exercise the next time you're worrying about an upcoming event. Before the event, make a note here of what you are worried will happen and how you think you will feel. Then, when it's over, add in what actually happened and how you actually felt. Treat it like a debrief report – which means sticking to the facts and only the facts. Now look at how the prediction compares to the outcome.

If you find similarities then you know that you have a solid basis to work from and can think about how you might support yourself for next time. However, if you find differences then you can use this data to soothe anxiety in the future. In particular, see if you can spot any thinking errors. Remember, your anxious part is just trying to help. But if it's using faulty assumptions to make predictions you now have the experience to begin to teach it differently.

PREDICTION

OUTCOME

REMINDERS

When we're feeling anxious our perspective shifts, our attention is drawn to what we're worried about or what's causing us stress, and we can lose sight of things that we might know to be true when we are in a more relaxed state. For instance, when we're anxious at work we might feel we need to keep focused on the problem when in fact a short walk would help us relax and we would return better able to tackle the problem.

We can forget about:

techniques that have been
helpful in the past

people who we can talk to
about our worries

how our thinking errors skew our
perspective on things

past outcomes and any predictive
errors we tend to make

how the sensation of anxiety will pass

Use the page opposite to make notes of those
things that you'd like to remind yourself of when
you're feeling anxious. Make it simple, persuasive
and compassionate. You know how best speak to
yourself when you're anxious. Use that knowledge to
communicate in a way that you're most likely to be
able to listen to and feel encouraged by. Then, when
you're next feeling anxious turn back to this page
and see if you can take your own advice.

RESOURCES

Samaritans: For anyone who is struggling, feels overwhelmed or needs a listening ear, 24 hours a day, 365 days a year. Visit **www.samaritans.org** or call **116 123**.

Anxiety UK: Offers support for people struggling with anxiety. Visit **www.anxietyuk.org.uk** or call **03444 775 774** (Monday to Friday 9.30 a.m. to 5.30 p.m.).

MIND: Provides advice and support via their website **www.mind.org.uk** and their infoline. Call **0300 123 3393** (Monday to Friday, 9 a.m. to 6 p.m., except bank holidays).

No Panic: Offers a helpline for people struggling with anxiety. Visit **www.nopanic.org.uk** or call **0300 772 9844** (10 a.m. to 10 p.m.).

SANE: Provides information, support and services for anyone affected by mental health problems. Visit **www.sane.org.uk** or call **0300 304 7000** (4 p.m. to 10 p.m.).

GP: If you need further support, your GP is a great place to start. They will guide you towards a range of resources and help you to make decisions about what is best for you.

BACP: If you'd like to pursue therapy, the British Association for Counselling and Psychotherapy offer a directory of qualified therapists. Visit **www.bacp.co.uk/search/Therapists**.

If you are in crisis don't hesitate to reach out. You can phone **111** or go straight to A&E for immediate help.

ALSO AVAILABLE

ISBN:9781782438007

ISBN:9781789292688

ISBN:9781912785384

ISBN:9781912785582

ISBN:9781789292626

ISBN:9781912785414